what counts

WIN WINS @ WORK™

how forward-thinking
leaders recognize and
reward employees

FranklinCovey.

Other Books from Franklin Covey

Warriors@Work: What the Smartest Business Leaders Are Saying
The 7 Habits of Highly Effective People
The 7 Habits of Highly Effective Families
The 7 Habits of Highly Effective Teens
The 7 Habits of Highly Effective Teens Journal
Daily Reflections for Highly Effective People
Living the 7 Habits
Choice: Choosing the Proactive Life You Want to Live
Renewal: Nourishing Heart, Mind, Body, and Soul
Loving Reminders for Kids
Loving Reminders for Couples
Loving Reminders for Families
Loving Reminders Teen to Teen
Quotes and Quips

Franklin Covey
2200 West Parkway Boulevard
Salt Lake City, Utah 84119-2099

This book is the proprietary work of Franklin Covey Co.
Many terms in this book, including the title, are trademarks of Franklin Covey Co.

Concept by Cheryl Kerzner
Written and compiled by Debra Harris
Book design by David Volsic
Manufactured in United States of America
ISBN 1-929494-07-6

RECOGNITION

PRAISE

GRATITUDE

PERSONALIZATION

ENTHUSIASM

CREATIVITY

EMPOWERMENT

CELEBRATIONS

REWARDS

AWARDS

INTRODUCTION

Brains, like hearts, go where they're appreciated.

ROBERT MCNAMARA

No employee wants to do a so-so job. They want to excel at work, add value to the company, and be recognized. Although this sounds like a no-brainer, many managers are too busy to realize the power that recognizing excellence on the job has on the human psyche. Especially in light of the competitive nature of keeping and compensating the best players.

Showing appreciation in today's fast-paced, ever-changing business environment has nothing to do with expensive gifts, lavish awards, or time-consuming celebrations. It's all about recognizing good work as it is happening, giving praise on the fly, and staying informally connected with coworkers and management. All it takes is the desire to encourage higher levels of performance from employees and a few simple and inexpensive ways to do it.

This book is written specifically for managers and executives who are looking for easy, creative ways to recognize great work, congratulate, encourage, motivate, thank, or provide feedback in an instant.

It gets right to the point with insightful quotes, doable ideas, practical tips, fun suggestions, and motivating sound bites from some of the most forward-thinking business leaders and recognition experts in the world. It is a valuable resource to show managers what they can do to treat employees as the company's most valuable assets. It also demonstrates what techniques have worked successfully for other organizations as well.

For those companies that still rely on the occasional pat on the back or mundane company banquet to keep employees motivated and excited about their jobs, this is your wake-up call. Because recognizing and rewarding employees isn't an option anymore. It's a necessity.

RECOGNITION

If you adopt a pattern of life that focuses on

GOLDEN EGGS

and neglects the goose, you will soon be without the asset that produces golden eggs. On the other hand, if you only take care of the goose with no aim toward the golden eggs, you soon won't have the wherewithal to feed yourself or the goose.

STEPHEN R. COVEY

The 7 Habits
of Highly Effective
Employee Recognition

1. **Be timely.** Don't wait. Praise should be given as soon as possible after the action or achievement occurs.

2. **Begin with proportion in mind.** In other words, don't give someone a roundtrip ticket to Paris for a good attendance record.

3. **Put specifics first.** Get to the point and identify the positive behavior immediately. Don't weigh down your praise with "setting the stage" rhetoric or beating around the bush.

4. **Think individual-individual.** Recognize the individuals who took the positive action. If the action was the work of a group, first recognize the individuals who were most instrumental and then recognize the group as a whole.

5. **Seek first to listen.** Get feedback from coworkers for additional praise for the individual. Peer recognition can be more rewarding than just a pat on the back from the big boss in many cases.

6. **Be sincere.** Be sincere and show your employees that you care, otherwise the recognition does more harm than good.

7. **Sharpen up on the personal.** The recognition should ultimately reflect the recipient's personality. Some people like to be recognized in public, others prefer a more private setting, while others would be happy with a personalized note or card.

WIN-WIN

Start an Annual Recognition Day. Have individuals and teams describe their achievements to other employees and their families. You'd be surprised at how often others don't have a clue what everyone does. Hearing about their own achievements from their peers builds pride and loyalty that perks from the top just can't beat.

Quick,
what recognition have you done in the past that gets the most positive response?

If your reason for establishing recognition and reward programs is to improve performance, it's not enough just to set goals for your employees and then wait until reward time to see if they've met them. Managers need to keep up with employees' progress toward goals, facilitate their access to resources, and guide them toward solutions to problems that block their progress. Your objective should be to have all your employees meet their goals and earn their rewards.

DONNA DEEPROSE

WIN-WIN

Recognize special events. Use your company or division newsletter to announce events such as marriages, births, service anniversaries, or graduations.

WINNER'S CIRCLE

At Autodesk, a leading developer of computer-aided software, employees are allowed to bring their dogs to work, may dress casually every day, and receive six-week paid sabbaticals every four years. On top of that, employees work in beautiful Marin County, California.

As you work with others, recognize that all people, whether leaders or followers, have some things in common:

They like to feel special, so sincerely compliment them.

They want a better tomorrow, so show them hope.

They desire direction, so navigate for them.

They are selfish, so speak to their needs first.

They get low emotionally, so encourage them.

They want success, so help them win.

JOHN. C. MAXWELL

leadership
is action,
not position.

D.H. MCGANNON

Be a generous leader. Give your time and efforts to add value to others. The one piece of advice which will contribute to making you a better leader, will provide you with great happiness and will advance your career more than any other advice...and it doesn't call for a special personality or any certain chemistry...and any one of you can do it. And that advice is: You must care.

LIEUTENANT GENERAL MELVIN ZAIS

WIN-WIN

Take two employees to lunch each month. Get feedback from them about how they would improve things if they could. Allow them to offer suggestions and ideas without judgment or disapproval. Thank them for their responses. You never know what new ideas can come out of listening to employees in a casual setting.

when was the
last time you
recognized
someone on
the spot for
his or her
contributions?

WINNER'S CIRCLE

Finovia Group, a financial group based in Phoenix, Arizona, offers a spectacular array of benefits for its employees, including $3,000 a year per child for college tuition, 500 stock options upon hiring, a concierge service, and free on-site massage.

top 10 behaviors
that deserve recognition

1. Learning new skills

2. Pitching in to help a coworker

3. Mediating a conflict

4. Volunteering for grunge work

5. Giving a customer extra attention

6. Mentoring a new employee

7. Tackling a problem a fresh way

8. Maintaining perfect attendance

9. Adapting willingly to change

10. Cross-training another employee

i've always been
a sucker
for attention.

CUBA GOODING JR.

PRAISE

The more deeply you understand other

PEOPLE

the more you will appreciate them, the more reverent you

will feel about them. To touch the soul of another human

being is to walk on holy ground.

STEPHEN R. COVEY

what you
praise you
increase.

CATHERINE PONDER

what every genuine philosopher (every genuine man, in fact) craves most is praise, although the philosophers generally call it "recognition"!

WILLIAM JAMES

if

you want employees to improve,
let them overhear
the nice things you say
about them to others.

HAIM GINOTT

One of the best things you can do for people—which also attracts them to you—is to expect the best of them. I call it putting a "10" on everyone's head. It helps others think more highly of themselves and at the same time, it also helps you. According to Jacques Weisel, "A survey of one hundred self-made millionaires showed only one common denominator. These highly successful men and women could only see the good in people."

JOHN C. MAXWELL

Whenever I meet someone, I try to imagine him wearing an invisible sign that says: make me feel important. I respond to this sign immediately, and it works wonders...I think it's essential that every manager remember that invisible sign:

make me feel important.

MARY KAY ASH

expect to find
the best
and you will.

WINNER'S CIRCLE

Union Pacific Resources, a Texas-based oil and gas drilling
company, reimburses childcare costs when employees who are
parents travel on company business.

do you set clear and specific goals?

if you don't, you can't complain when others

don't meet your standards.

be clear about
your expectations.

work

is not all about
work.

GRATITUDE

always treat your

EMPLOYEES

exactly as you want them to treat your best customers.

STEPHEN R. COVEY

Opening up is harder for some people than for others, but major psychotherapy is not required here. It starts with what Robert Fulghum pointed out some years ago in his book *Everything I Ever Needed to Know I Learned in Kindergarten*, the little reminder pinned to the wall where you're sure to see it every morning when you come to work: "Remember to say thank you!"

JAMES M. KOUZES AND BARRY Z. POSNER

WIN-WIN

Allow courtesy time off. Grant employees an afternoon off, or even a day or two of leave with pay for special, personal events in their lives. This will give your employees the message that you value what is important in their lives. Besides, they'll more than make up for lost time on the job.

WINNER'S CIRCLE

Original Copy Centers, in Cleveland, Ohio, publishes a company yearbook. The execution is simple—everybody fills out questionnaires about their favorite music, ideal weekend, biggest challenges, and best childhood memory. Other fill-in-the-blanks: "What I really like about my job and my role at Original." The book devotes a full page to each person's quotes, which run alongside a photo.

WIN-WIN

Create a "year in review" book. Take photos and keep notes of

your team's proudest achievements during the year and present

it to the department at a holiday party or an annual event.

WIN-WIN

Construct a bulletin board at your place of business to recognize employees and their customer service efforts through letters, memos, pictures, thank-you cards, and other methods. Be creative.

WINNER'S CIRCLE

When you walk into IBM's New York Financial Center, the first thing you see is a floor-to-ceiling bulletin board with glossy photos of every person in the branch. A sign above the board states: New York Financial...the difference is people.

how have you demonstrated your

appreciation in the past?

what can you do to improve?

never miss an
opportunity
to tell an employee

how valuable he or she is

to the company.

The person who works well four days out of five ought to be praised four times as often as he's dumped on. But guess what. That's exactly the opposite of what happens. The 80 percent of the time that he works well will simply go without comment because that's what he's supposed to be doing.

FRAN TARKENTON

just say it.

thanks, that is.

[and do it often.]

patting the back
knocks a chip
off the shoulder.

MURIEL SOLOMON

Thank you isn't just for people who report to you. It's the reward you have the power (and the resources) to give to your boss and your peers in the organization when they do something of value to you. It's also a tool for influencing changes in their behavior. By thanking them specifically when you catch them doing something that is helpful to you, you give them the information and motivation they need to continue behaving in a way that's best for you. Your boss needs to be appreciated just as much as you.

bosses
need
praise
too.

PERSONALIZATION

When we really, deeply understand each other,

WE OPEN THE DOOR

to creative solutions and third alternatives. Our differences are no longer stumbling blocks to communication and progress. Instead, they become the stepping stone to synergy.

STEPHEN R. COVEY

WIN-WIN

Develop a unique Winners' Trophy. Choose deserving employees whenever the occasion arises and give them the trophy to put in their cubicle or office for a day. Have employees pass it on to each other.

get to know your employees.
what do they do in their spare time?
what hobbies and sports do they enjoy?

WIN-WIN

Write a family recognition letter. Recognize an employee's family by sending a letter of appreciation when their family member has had to work long hours. Thank them for their understanding and patience. Don't forget to tell them how valuable their family member is to the company.

WINNER'S CIRCLE

The recognition and motivation program at Monsanto was in a rut. So the idea of a book was tossed around. Hence, *The Master Salesman* was developed. It contained the wit and wisdom of their top salespeople. The book idea has been imitated by other companies with great success. In fact, *The Master Salesman* is often used in training programs at many major corporations.

The acknowledgement of effort has to be tailor-made. People pick up on canned compliments, especially if they hear the same things being said to other people. Nothing is more effective than sincere, accurate praise, and nothing is more lame than a cookie-cutter compliment.

BILL WALSH

do you **personally acknowledge your employees**
for their contributions?

Next time you recognize an employee, tell a story about the person. Ideally, it would be about the performance you are recognizing, but it could also be something more personal, like your impression the day you hired the individual.

WIN-WIN

Design a logo or develop a slogan that is fitting of your company or department. At Dahlin Smith White, an advertising agency in Salt Lake City, Utah, the initials of the company name DSW were designed into a logo with the slogan "Do Something Wild." With that one Win-Win, the entire company culture was defined. And the logo appeared on everything from self-promotion ads to t-shirts to leather jackets.

WIN-WIN

Call an employee into your office just to give a more personalized thank you for a job well done.

The horizon is not where the sky comes down. We set our own boundaries. We have the making of our own horizons. We do not have to live in walled-in spaces.

GROVE PATTERSON

In experiment after experiment, workers who thought they were doing better did better. In one experiment, ten people were given puzzles to solve. They were all given fictitious results. Half were told they had done well, the other half were told they had done poorly. They were then given a second test and this time they all did as well or as poorly as they were told they did on the first test.

WARREN BENNIS

WIN-WIN

Whatever you do, personalize your recognition. Don't just hand over a certificate with the CEO's faded and overly-copied signature. [Give birthday and service anniversary cards to employees personally signed by the chairman or CEO.]

remember
that a **man's name**
is, to him, the sweetest and
most important sound
in any language.

DALE CARNEGIE

ENTHUSIASM

Sometimes the most

PROACTIVE

thing we can do is to just genuinely smile. Happiness, like

unhappiness, is a proactive choice.

STEPHEN R. COVEY

Apathy can be overcome by enthusiasm, and enthusiasm can be aroused by two things: first, an idea which takes the imagination by storm; and second, a definite, intelligible plan for carrying that idea into action.

ARNOLD TOYNBEE

be enthusiastic or settle for less. your employees will mirror your enthusiasm or lack of it in their work.

WIN-WIN

Write a note of congratulations or send an e-mail to someone who has done a good job. Make copies and send it to his or her coworkers and supervisors or upper management.

enthusiasm...

spells the difference

between mediocrity

and accomplishment.

NORMAN VINCENT PEALE

WIN-WIN

Develop a wellness program. If you don't have an in-house fitness facility, make arrangements with a local health club. Give free memberships to employees. Get everyone fired up to work out together. Join them and watch the enthusiasm flow.

WINNER'S CIRCLE

Harley Davidson rewards employees $100 every three months for perfect attendance, caters luncheons honoring production achievements, and provides interest-free loans of up to $3,000 to buy a personal computer.

failure is
the path
of least
persistence.

ANONYMOUS

If we have talent and cannot use it, we have failed. If we have a talent and use only half of it, we have partly failed. If we have a talent and learn somehow to use all of it, we have gloriously succeeded, and won a satisfaction and a triumph few individuals ever know.

THOMAS WOLFE

WIN-WIN

Make Wednesday afternoon snack time. Buy a big bag of assorted candy and healthy snacks. Walk around to your staff members passing out treats. It's a great way to interact and gives employees a little boost midweek when the slump can set in.

if you're not failing at some things,
you're not risking enough.

GORDON WILSON

the difference between

ordinary and extraordinary

is that little extra.

WIN-WIN

Designate a Parking Spot of Honor. Recognize a different employee each month for exceptional work by allowing the staff member to park in the assigned Spot of Honor.

WIN-WIN

Start a mentor program. Assign staff members as mentors to new employees or team members. Encourage mentors to maintain an informal relationship with the new employee for his or her first six months on the job.

CREATIVITY

Ineffective people live day by day with unused

POTENTIAL

They experience synergy only in small, peripheral ways in their lives. But creative experiences can be produced regularly, consistently, almost daily in people's lives. It requires enormous personal security and openness and a spirit of adventure.

STEPHEN R. COVEY

The most exciting breakthrough of the 21st century will occur not because of technology, but because of an expanding concept of what it means to be human.

JOHN NAISBITT

can you do the unexpected? if not,

loosen up.

it's not a button-down world anymore.

WIN-WIN

During a team get-together, ask each person to perform a song, tell a story, write an ad, or act out a skit that personifies another member of the group. Have everyone guess whom the performance portrays. Make sure performances are geared around what the person does best at work.

creative leaders find ways of stepping into the shoes of other people and asking, "how would i feel and what would i want if i were this person?"

GAY HENDRICKS AND KATE LUDEMAN

glorious opportunities
do not come to those
who are afraid to think
outside the box.

WINNER'S CIRCLE

According to Bob Nelson's *1001 Ways To Recognize and Reward Employees*, Hallmark Greeting Cards in Kansas City, Missouri, bankrolls a creativity center stocked with clay, paint, and other art materials to help the company's creative staff think up ideas for the 21,000 different greeting card designs it publishes each year. Hallmark's staff is energized by the freedom to create, and the company reaps the benefit of exciting new ideas.

you shouldn't be frightened
by **new** ideas.
you should be
more frightened of old ones.

trial and error is the secret sauce of the creative process. when we find out what doesn't work, we eventually discover what does.

WIN-WIN

Hold a Friday Surprise. Do something fun with your staff like ordering pizza for lunch or going on an impromptu picnic. It's a great way to recognize employees for working hard or just for hanging in there during a tough week.

WINNER'S CIRCLE

According to *Industry Week* magazine, Odetics, the robot maker based in Anaheim, California, is "the wackiest place to work in the United States." The company's employees frequently take part in all kinds of nutty, routine-breaking activities, including telephone booth stuffing and a '50s day, featuring a sock hop that starts at 6:00 a.m. The company also sponsors programs in stress management, accupressure, and yoga, which help employees to relax while unleashing their creativity.

the most important thing i learned from big companies is that creativity gets stifled when everyone's got to follow the rules.

DAVID KELLEY

EMPOWERMENT

The imagination can be used to achieve the fleeting

SUCCESS

that comes when a person is focused on material gain or on

"what's in it for me." But I believe the higher use for imagination

is in harmony with the use of conscience to transcend self

and create a life of contribution based on unique purpose

and on the principles that govern interdependent reality.

STEPHEN R. COVEY

Wherever you find a strong culture built around strong values, whether they are about superior quality, innovation, customer service, distinctiveness in design, respect for others, or just plain fun, you also find endless examples of leaders who personally live the values. Yes, it may emanate from the top, but a culture is sustained over time because everyone becomes a leader; everyone sets the examples.

JAMES M. KOUZES AND BARRY Z. POZNER

the best companies
assume that each individual
wants to make a difference in
the world and be respected.
is that a surprise?

PAUL AMES

WIN-WIN

As a token of your appreciation, send a valued employee to a training course or seminar to increase performance and prepare the person for a more sophisticated set of goals.

there are low spots in our lives, but there are also high spots, and most of them have come through encouragement from someone else.

GEORGE M. ADAMS

WIN-WIN

Develop an Extra Mile award and give it to employees for extraordinary accomplishments during the year. Make it a coveted award that is not given lightly.

People want to feel empowered to find better ways to do things and to take responsibility for their own environment. Allowing them to do this has had a big impact on how they do their jobs, as well as on their satisfaction with the company.

JAMES BERDAHL

do you

let people know you have

confidence

in their abilities?

WINNER'S CIRCLE

MBNA, a credit card issuer from Wilmington, Delaware, awards $15,000 per year in its Suggestion Program to the individual or team with the year's best idea. They also give new parents $2,500, which goes toward the child's education.

when you find someone
doing **small things** well,
put him or her in charge
of **bigger things.**

H. JACKSON BROWNE JR.

WIN-WIN

Empower your employees to develop their own reward programs. Allow them to contribute their Win-Win ideas. This technique allows employees to take ownership of the program as well as devlop a better understanding of what is expected and how to get there. And let the innovative Win-Wins flow.

people
will support
that which
they help
to create.

MARY KAY ASH

to empower others
is ultimately
to empower oneself.

MARY ELIZABETH SCHLAYER

finding the right work
is like discovering your
own soul in the world.

THOMAS MOORE

CELEBRATIONS

Without involvement, there is no

COMMITMENT

Mark it down, asterisk it, circle it, underline it. No

involvement, no commitment.

STEPHEN R. COVEY

A leader who ignores or impedes organizational ceremonies and considers them frivolous or not cost-effective is ignoring the rhythms of history and our collective conditioning. Ceremonies are the punctuation marks that make sense of the passage of time; without them, there are no beginnings and endings. Life becomes an endless series of Wednesdays.

DAVID CAMPBELL

TOP CELEBRATION SONGS

1. New Attitude
2. All Fired Up
3. The Best
4. Celebration
5. I'm So Excited
6. The Power of Love
7. Ghostbusters
8. Winners
9. Victory
10. Shout
11. Man in the Mirror
12. We Are the Champions
13. Danger Zone
14. The Greatest Love of All
15. Footloose
16. One Moment in Time
17. I Heard It Through the Grapevine
18. You Got It
19. Wind Beneath My Wings
20. 40 Hour Week
21. Don't Worry Be Happy
22. We Are Family
23. Nine to Five
24. Flashdance... What a Feeling
25. The Way You Do Things
26. Put a Little Love in Your Heart
27. Taking It to the Streets
28. Takin' Care of Business
29. You Ain't Seen Nothing Yet
30. The Heat Is On

Create a collegial, supportive, zany, laughter-filled environment where folks support one another and office "politics" are as absent as is possible in a human (i.e. imperfect) enterprise.

TOM PETERS

WIN-WIN

Hold a Peer Party. Once a month bring in pastries or cake and ice cream. Have employees vote for a peer who has contributed the most during the month.

WIN-WIN

Establish a Breakfast Club. Meet at your favorite restaurant, funky coffee shop, or even Starbucks. Keep it casual or have an informal idea exchange or breakfast meeting.

WINNER'S CIRCLE

According to *1001 Ways To Recognize and Reward Employees* by Bob Nelson, Physio-Control, a producer of cardiac care equipment in Redmond, Washington, treats employees who attend fourth-quarter meetings to a pancake breakfast. The employees are honored and energized by the event as well as the special efforts of senior management who literally serve them breakfast.

what can
you celebrate
this week?

WIN-WIN

Establish a free First Friday Lunch for employees. Bring in food or go to a different restaurant on the first Friday of each month to celebrate—what else? Friday!

WINNER'S CIRCLE

According to *1001 Ways To Recognize and Reward Employees* by Bob Nelson, cofounder Jerry Greenfield of Ben & Jerry's Homemade Ice Cream in Waterbury, Vermont, coordinates such special events as "National Clash Dressing Day" and "Elvis Day."

There is a great creative void in most of corporate America. When you inject a level of humor and playfulness, employees find a common ground. They're reminded that they're all working on the same side.

CARL ROBINSON

WINNER'S CIRCLE

Celebrations are big at Valassis Communications, a newspaper insert printer. When the stock hit a target price, employees partied at an airport hangar and were given flights on a vintage B-11 bomber. The company also offers an on-site hairstylist, manicurist, and doctor. New parents receive an infant car seat.

REWARDS

You can buy people's hands, but you can't buy their

HEARTS

Their hearts are where their their loyalty is. You can buy their backs, but you can't buy their brains. That's where their creativity is, their ingenuity, their resourcefulness.

STEPHEN R. COVEY

a reward is a special gain for
special achievements,
    a treat for doing something
above-and-beyond.

ROSABETH MOSS KANTER

WINNER'S CIRCLE

When Levi Strauss, headquartered in San Francisco, California, reached $1 billion in sales, its executives gave out more than $2 million worth of stock and cash to employees as rewards. They did it again four years later when sales passed the $2 billion mark.

men and women
want to do a good job,
and if they are provided the proper
environment, **they will do so.**

BILL HEWLETT

WIN-WIN

Give someone a complete car detailing for working long hours.

Make it easy on the employee and have the detailers do the

work in your company parking lot. Or have them pick up and

deliver the car after the job is completed off-site.

WIN-WIN

Give valued employees a subscription to the publication of

their choice from your list of approved titles. It doesn't have to

just be business-related magazines. If they are golf nuts, let

them choose a golf magazine. Remember that recognition is all

about personalizing.

everyone works smarter
when there's something
 in it for them.

MICHAEL LEBOEUF

One reason food is a good motivator is that it provides the winner with an experience he or she can share with family and friends. Food is a social gift.

JEFFREY GIBEAULT

WIN-WIN

For impromptu gift-giving, keep a grab bag of prizes handy.

They can be anything from a gift certificate for lunch to a

day-off coupon. Let the recipients choose their own reward.

five most important words:

i am proud of you!

four most important words:

what is your opinion?

three most important words:

if you please.

two most important words:

thank you.

one most important word:

you.

WIN-WIN

Is an employee a collector of any kind? Be on the lookout for specific items that would personalize recognition and add to his or her collection. Fly fishing aficionado? Give a subscription to *Fly-Fishing* magazine or a box of favorite flies. You get the picture. You're only limited by your imagination or your info-gathering skills.

WIN-WIN

Give employees the latest book that pertains to their area of expertise or business in general. Write a note in the front of the book and sign your name.

Next to physical survival,

THE GREATEST NEED

of a human being is psychological survival—to be understood,

to be affirmed, to be validated, to be appreciated.

STEPHEN R. COVEY

WIN-WIN

Host a Guess Who party. Have your employees bring in their

baby pictures or high school photos to post in a visible location.

Have your employees or group submit their guesses as to who's

who. The person with the most correct answers wins.

giving
is the highest level of
living.

JOHN C. MAXWELL

if

you are going to dangle
something in front of them,
why limit yourself to carrots?

WIN-WIN

Invent an unusual, creative name that has meaning to your company or department and turn it into an award. For instance, The Swooping Eagle Award—given to the person who got dumped on the most during the week and needs a little support to get back into the swing of things.

S hort of mind reading, how is a manager supposed to figure out what reward will please a person and what might do harm? Following are some specific suggestions and some guidelines that should help keep you out of trouble, according to *How To Recognize and Reward Employees* by Donna Deeprose.

1. **Ask.** That's the most obvious solution. Privately tell the person that you are very pleased with his work and explain the reward you had in mind, making it clear that your idea is not yet cast in stone. Let the person know that what you really want is to give him something he values. Then ask for a reaction to your proposal.

2. **Give options.** If you give a few suggestions, the employee can pick one without fear of offending you.

3. **Observe.** What makes the person smile? What does the individual take pleasure in during the workday? What does she talk about during her free time?

4. **Confirm your observations.** Sometimes it is appropriate to ask a good friend of the individual or even to call up a close family member.

5. **Avoid anything that might embarrass the person.** You should know an individual well enough before presenting a joke award, staging a ceremonial "roast," putting the person on the spot with a call for a speech, or even asking the person to describe her accomplishments to upper management.

6. **If you don't get the desired response, do not make judgments.** How the person responds to your show of appreciation doesn't change the fact that he did a good job and is capable of doing so again. As long as the person is in the right job, someone whose pleasure at work comes from camaraderie with coworkers can be just as productive as someone with a strong desire to move up the corporate ladder.

7. **Don't be reluctant to try again if your first award doesn't inspire cartwheels.** You won't lose face by asking, "How can I show my appreciation in a way that is more meaningful to you than last time when I put you on the spot in front of everybody?"

gift certificates
beyond the ordinary

When buying a gift certificate, personalize it according to the taste of the individual. And think beyond your local geographic area. You can go virtually anywhere online to find exactly what you're looking for. Here's a list of top quality gift certificate providers for hassle-free employee incentives. Call for more information on their specific programs.

Foot Locker   1-800-690-5996

Movado Watches   1-800-392-3631
www.movado.com

Blockbuster GiftCard®   1-888-313-2234

Marriott Incentive Programs   1-800-835-7754
www.marriott.com/incentives

1-800-FLOWERS   1-800-FLOWERS
1-800-FLOWERS.com

Warner Bros. Studio Stores   1-800-574-9449

Eddie Bauer   1-800-552-8943
www.eddiebauer.com

Spiegel Rewards 1-800-982-5664
www.spiegelrewards.com

The Home Depot 1-770-384-4330

Herrington The Enthusiasts Catalog 1-603-425-6620

Crutchfield Audio/Video catalog 1-888-809-5145
www.crutchfield.com/incentives

Cracker Barrel Old Country Store 1-800-576-7693
www.crackerbarrel.com

RCA Quickpick Catalog 1-800-486-2258
www.rca.com

Holland America Incentive
Cruise Planning Kit 1-877-SAIL ext.404

Virtual Vineyard 1-888-WINE-789
www.virtualvineyard.com

Crate & Barrel Corporate Sales 1-800-717-1112

Stock Yards of Chicago 1-800-621-3687

Omaha Steaks 1-800-228-2480

1-800-GIFT CERTIFICATE 1-800-GIFT CERTIFICATE
www.800giftcertificate.com

the high-impact way
to recognize and reward employees

The Win-Wins@Work product line from Franklin Covey is the high-impact way to help managers recognize great work, congratulate, encourage, motivate, thank, or provide feedback in an instant. Maybe that's why it's generating so much excitement as one of the most innovative employee recognition programs to date.

Other Win-Wins@Work™ Products by Franklin Covey

Warriors@Work: What the Smartest Business Leaders Are Saying

Bragging Rights™ Messages

Congrats Pack™

You Rock Cards™

Win-Wins@Work Magnet

Win-Wins@Work Bookmark

For more information or to order, call Franklin Covey at 1-800-952-6839

About Franklin Covey

Franklin Covey is the world's leading time management and life leadership company. Based on proven principles, our services and products are used by more than 15 million people worldwide. We work with a wide variety of clients—Fortune 500 material—as well as smaller companies, communities, and organizations. You may know us from our world-renowned Franklin Planner or any of our books in the 7 Habits series. By the way, Franklin Covey books have sold over 15 million copies worldwide—over 1 1/2 million each year. But what you may not know about Franklin Covey is that we also offer leadership training, motivational workshops, personal coaching, audio and video tapes, and *Priorities*™ magazine, just to name a few. If you want more information, see us on the web at www.franklincovey.com or visit a Franklin Covey store near you.

Franklin Covey

2200 West Parkway Boulevard

Salt Lake City, Utah 84119-2331

www.franklincovey.com

1-800-952-6839

International (801) 229-1333

Permissions and Acknowledgements

Boone, Louis.E. *Quotable Business*. Random House, 1999.

Collins, James C., and Jerry I. Porras. *Built to Last: Successful Habits of Visionary Companies*. HarperCollins, 1997.

Covey, Stephen R. *Daily Reflections for Highly Effective People*. William Morrow and Company, 1999.

Deal, Terrence E., and M. K. Key. *Corporate Celebration: Play, Purpose, and Profit at Work*. Berrett-Koehler Publishers, 1998.

Deep, Sam, and Lyle Sussman. *Smart Moves for People in Charge*. Addison-Wesley, 1995.

Deeprose, Donna. *How to Recognize & Reward Employees*. AMACOM, 1994.

Downs, Alan. *Seven Miracles of Management*. Prentice Hall, 1998.

Griffith, Joe. *Speaker's Library of Business Stories, Anecdotes, and Humor*. Prentice Hall, 1990.

Hiam, Alexander. *Motivating & Rewarding Employees: New and Better Ways to Inspire Your People*. Adams Media Corporation, 1999.

Hyland, Bruce, and Merle Yost. *Reflections for Managers*. McGraw-Hill, 1994.

Kaye, Beverly, and Sharon Jordan-Evans. *Love 'Em or Lose 'Em: Getting Good People to Stay*. Berrett-Koehler Publishers, 1999.

Kouzes, James M., and Barry Z. Posner. *Encouraging the Heart: A Leader's Guide to Rewarding and Recognizing Others*. Jossey-Bass, 1999.

Maxwell, John C. *The 21 Indispensable Qualities of a Leader*. Thomas Nelson, 1999.

Nelson, Bob. *1001 Ways to Energize Employees*. Workman Publishing Company, 1997.

——— *1001 Ways to Reward Employees*. Workman Publishing Company, 1994.

Pacetta, Frank, and Roger Gittines. *Don't Fire Them, Fire Them Up: Motivate Yourself and Your Team*. Simon & Schuster, 1994.

Peters, Tom. *The Circle of Innovation: You Can't Shrink Your Way to Greatness*. Vintage Books, 1999.

Donna Deeprose quotes reprinted from *How to Recognize & Reward Employees* by Donna Deeprose, et al. Copyright ©1994 AMACOM, a division of American Management Association International. Reprinted by permission of AMACOM, a division of American Management Association International, New York, NY. All rights reserved. http://www.mamnet.org.